To the 2 cutest nephews
in the world . . .
happy happy birthday
and I will see you in
Santa Fe !

Love,
Aunt Marsha

Donation 4/01

Library of Congress Cataloging-in-Publication Data
Moss, Jeffrey.
The Sesame Street Book of Poetry / by Jeff Moss ; illustrated
by Bruce McNally.
p.   cm.
Summary: A collection of short poems featuring Jim Henson's
Sesame Street Muppets.
ISBN 0-679-80774-8 (trade) — ISBN 0-679-90774-2 (lib. bdg.)
1. Puppets—Juvenile poetry. 2. Children's poetry, American.
3. Recitations—Juvenile literature. [1. Puppets—Poetry.
2. American poetry.] I. McNally, Bruce, ill.
II. Children's Television Workshop.
III. Sesame Street (television program). IV. Title.
PS3563.O88458S47 1992
811'.54—dc20
90-8994

Manufactured in the United States of America

10   9   8   7   6   5   4   3   2   1

The Sesame Street
Book of Poetry

by Jeff Moss

illustrated by Bruce McNally

Random House/Children's Television Workshop

Contents

Thirty-Two Cracks
in the Sidewalk

There are thirty-two cracks in the sidewalk
From the end of the block to my door.
There are seventeen cracks to the mailbox
And twenty-six cracks to the store.
There is one thing I'll always be sure of
Wherever I happen to roam,
There are thirty-two cracks in the sidewalk
From the end of the block to my home.

Happy

Happy can start in the tip of my toes,
And I can go with it wherever it goes.
From the tip of my toes to the top of my knees
To a spot in my tummy that nobody sees.
Then up to my chest and my chin and from there
To the edge of my ears and the ends of my hair.
Happy can fly till it reaches the sky,
All the way to the moon without telling me why.
Happy can start in the tip of my toes,
And I can go with it wherever it goes.

A Monster Must Have
Spilled My Milk

A monster must have spilled my milk,
He must have hit my cup.
He must have knocked it on the floor
And didn't clean it up.
So when my mother sees it
I'm sure she will agree,
A monster must have spilled my milk,
It couldn't have been me.

Prairie Is Six

Prairie is six,
And she says she's all grown,
With a whole lot of things
She can do on her own.
She can write her own name.
She can tie her own shoe.
She can take her own bath.
She can add two and two.
She can do her own buttons
And pour her own juice.
She can wiggle her tooth
In the front where it's loose.
She's beginning to read.
She can brush her own hair.
She can help her mom pick out
The clothes that she'll wear.
(She says when she's seven,
She'll even be ready
For going to bed
With no night-light or teddy.)
Prairie is six,
And she says she's all grown,
With a whole lot of things
She can do all alone.

Six Sick Snuffle-upaguses

Six sick Snuffle-upaguses,
Sniffling and sneezy,
Had six stuffy snuffles,
So sneezing wasn't easy!

Noses

A nose can breathe.
A nose can smell.
A nose does those things
Very well.
There's one more thing
A nose can do.
And that is...
Ah...
    Ahh...
        Ahhh...
           AHCHOO!!!

Two-Headed Monster

I know a two-headed monster,
A very good friend of mine.
Whenever I ask him, "How are you?"
He answers, "I'm fine." "I'm fine."
Whenever we go out for ice cream,
He orders a big double scoop.
He uses two books when he's reading
And asks for two spoons with his soup.
Whenever we walk in the garden,
He loves to smell two different roses,
And he always carries two hankies
So that he can blow his two noses.

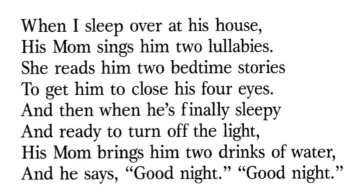

When I sleep over at his house,
His Mom sings him two lullabies.
She reads him two bedtime stories
To get him to close his four eyes.
And then when he's finally sleepy
And ready to turn off the light,
His Mom brings him two drinks of water,
And he says, "Good night." "Good night."

Still We Like
Each Other

Your fur is brown,
My fur is blue.
You love spaghetti,
I like carrot stew.
You visit museums,
I go to the zoo.
But still you like me,
And I like you.

14

Oscar's Poem

I am grouchy,
I am grumpy.
I like oatmeal
Cold and lumpy.
I hate ice cream,
I hate smiles.
I love trash
In great big piles.

I am grouchy,
I am grumpy.
I like car rides
Nice and bumpy.
One more thing
I'd like to say,
Read this poem and...
GO AWAY!!

I Wonder
Why I'm Purple

I wonder why I'm purple
Instead of green or red.
I wonder why I'm furry
And not all smooth instead.
I wonder why I'm Telly
Instead of Joe or Sam.
I wonder and I wonder
Why I'm all the things I am.

Monsters

Monsters can be just like you,
Riding their bikes or tying their shoe,
Big or little, happy or sad,
With brothers and sisters and Mom and Dad.
Monsters can be just like you,
So why can't kids be furry and blue?

Elmo, the Undersea Diver

Young Elmo McGyver, the undersea diver,
Prepared for a bath and a scrub.
But *squish* and *kerplunk*, his soap slipped and sunk,
So Elmo dove into the tub.

He dove very deep, where the sea horses sleep,
And soon swimming there by his side
Was a magical fish who asked, "What is your wish?"
"I must find my soap!" Elmo cried.

Said the fish, "Don't lose hope! We will soon find your soap.
Climb aboard, for we must take a trip
Far beyond the tail of the friendly blue whale
To the wreck of a pirate ship."

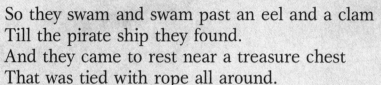

So they swam and swam past an eel and a clam
Till the pirate ship they found.
And they came to rest near a treasure chest
That was tied with rope all around.

They opened the treasure and much to their pleasure,
They found the soap inside.
Said the fish, "Glub-glub-glub. Now return to your tub."
And Elmo said, "Thanks for the ride."

Summer

I stand on the sand
At the edge of the beach
And put my toes right
Where the next wave will reach.

Autumn

All the leaves were green.
They changed to red and gold.
Now the leaves have fallen,
And the trees look sad and cold.

Winter

I went to bed one winter night.
When I woke up the street was white,
The cars were white, the trees were too.
(I'm awfully glad that snow's not blue.)

Spring

The first flower came
Where there used to be snow.
I'm glad that the flowers
Remembered to grow.

The Finny-Funny House

There's a finny-funny house
On Silly-Sally Lane,
Where the strangest things happen
That are hard to explain.

When you jump on a couch,
The couch says, "Ouch!"
If you stand on a chair,
It cries, "Not fair!"
If you slam a door,
It yells, "No more!"
If you bang on the ceilings,
You hurt their feelings.

There's a finny-funny house
On Silly-Sally Lane,
Where the strangest things happen
That are hard to explain.

I Met One Man upon the Street

I met **1** man upon the street.
He wore **2** shoes upon his feet.
Upon his head he wore **3** hats
And on a leash he held **4** cats.
Upon his fingers, **5** gold rings
And **6** balloons he held on strings.
He juggled **7** balls of blue.
Above his head **8** blackbirds flew.
He had **9** pockets in his pants.
And on his nose **10** fleas did dance.
We chatted for a day or so
Till it was time for him to go.
Then as we heard the church bells' chimes,
He said good-bye **11** times.

In

A bird flew in my window.
A bear walked in my door.
A mouse jumped in my pocket.
A frog hopped in my drawer.
A snake crawled in my closet.
And they all heard me shout,
"I do not want you in here!"
And so they all went out.

Out

Milk pours out of a bottle,
Rain falls out of the sky.
Smoke puffs out of a chimney,
Tears fall out of an eye.
Jokes jump out of my grandpa's mouth,
Hairs sprout out of his chin.
And out of my head this poem comes.
I wonder how it got in.

The Twiddlebug Ball

All the bugs came
To the Twiddlebug Ball—
Bumblebees, ladybugs,
Beetle-bugs, and all.
They heard Mr. Twiddlebug
Playing the fiddle-bug.
They saw Mrs. Twiddlebug
Dancing the diddle-bug.
They watched Tommy Twiddlebug
Cooking on the griddle-bug,

And heard Sally Twiddlebug
Asking a riddle-bug.
They danced through the evening
And sang through the night.
Not a bug flew home
Till the dawn's first light.
Bumblebees, ladybugs,
Beetle-bugs, and all
Had a buggy time
At the Twiddlebug Ball!

Last Night
I Ate a Triangle

Last night I ate a triangle,
And though it may sound strange,
Today I think I'll eat
Some squares and circles for a change.

Why eat a square and circle?
Well, a monster must be fed,
And my square and circle sandwich is
Baloney on white bread.

How did I eat a triangle?
In case you'd like to try,
Just gobble up one perfect piece
Of yummy pizza pie.

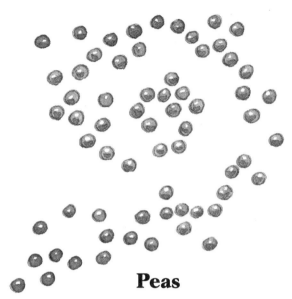

Peas

Each evening my dinner is great,
Because I have peas on my plate.
They are tasty and fun,
And I count every one.
Last night I munched seventy-eight.

Alive

How do you know if something's alive?
Well, here is how it goes:
You can be sure that something's alive
If it breathes and it eats and it grows.

Is a bear alive?
Is a chair alive?
(Well, it's clear that a chair
Doesn't breathe any air.)

Is a duck alive?
Is a truck alive?
(Well, everyone knows
That a truck never grows.)

Is a cat alive?
Is a hat alive?
(Well, it's plain that a hat
Doesn't eat and get fat.)

Is a shoe alive?
A kangaroo alive?
Is glue alive?
Are you alive?

Oh, how do you know if something's alive?
By now it is clear, I suppose:
You can be sure that something's alive
If it breathes and it eats and it grows.

Opposite Town

In Opposite Town
I've been told
Ice cream is hot,
Soup is cold.
Grandmas are young,
Babies are old
In Opposite Town,
I've been told.

Giraffes are short,
And frogs are tall.
A penny's big,
A mountain's small.
The floor is up,
The ceiling's down.
That's how things are
In Opposite Town.

In Opposite Town
I have found
Balls are square,
Books are round.
The sun is blue,
The sea is gold
In Opposite Town,
I've been told.

The Knee of a Flea

If I were as small as the knee of a flea,
I could fly through the sky on the back of a bee
And stop for a nap on the leaf of a tree,
If I were as small as the knee of a flea.

If I were as small as the eye of a fly,
I could jump in your pocket as you wandered by.
Then we'd have a secret, just you and I,
If I were as small as the eye of a fly.

31

As I Lay Sleeping

As I lay sleeping in the dark,
My dog woke up and gave a bark.
My dog woke up, imagine that.
He barked so loud he woke my cat.
My cat woke up and meowed, of course.
She meowed so loud she woke my horse.
My horse woke up, and what bad luck,
He neighed so loud he woke my duck.
My duck went quacking through the house.
She quacked so loud she woke my mouse.
My mouse woke up, and then somehow,
She squeaked so loud she woke my cow.
My cow woke up and she went "Moo!"
So loud she woke my kangaroo.
My kangaroo hopped around the floor.
She woke my lion who started to roar.
That roar woke up my bumblebee.
My bumblebee buzzed,
And that woke me!

My Baby Sister, Alice

I remember Alice
Before she learned to walk.
I remember Alice
Before she learned to talk.
My Mom remembers something
That's amazing if it's true:
Mom remembers *me*
Before I walked and talked, too.
(Does your Mom remember
The same thing about you?)

Why You Can't Play Alone on a Seesaw

You need a friend
On the other end.

33

The Cereal Box on the Shelf

How can I reach that cereal box
That's too high on the shelf?
Well, one way is: I could call Dad,
He's taller than myself.
Or I could get a ladder
And climb up to the top.
Or maybe I could reach it
With the handle of a mop.
Or how about a jet plane
To fly up in the sky?
And maybe I could grab the box
As I go zooming by.
There's one last thing I thought of
But it might be very slow—
I could stand right here and wait and wait
And wait...until I grow.

Learning to Ride My Bike

I tried and fell and tried and then
I tried once more and fell again.
I thought I'd never learn at all.
Each day I'd wobble, then I'd fall.
I couldn't ever get it right,
Just almost, nearly...but not quite.
Until one day I tried again,
I zigged and zagged and then...and then...
I pedaled once and then once more,
And it was different than before.
I pedaled but I didn't fall!
Somehow I stayed up straight and tall,
Riding, riding, on two wheels!
And I can tell you how it feels—
On the day I learned to ride,
I felt all strong and big inside.

Quiet

The whisper of a secret,
The humming of the bees,
A lullaby at bedtime
As wind blows through the trees.
The snowflakes falling softly,
Swirling to the ground.
Those things are quiet...
Shhh! Don't make a sound!

Loud

The banging of a trash can,
The honking in the street,
The roaring of a lion,
The stomping of your feet,
The booming of the thunder,
The yelling of a crowd—
All of those noises
Are sounds that are LOUD!

Worry

I worry that my fur's not straight
Or that my shoes aren't tied.
I worry playing hide-and-seek
I'll find no place to hide.

I worry that I might get lost
Out playing in the park.
I worry if my night-light breaks
I'll be stuck in the dark.

I worry that I might be late,
I know I'd better hurry.
Sometimes I worry oh so much
I'm worried that I worry.

The Dinner Adventure

I had an adventure at dinner,
Exploring new worlds was my plan.
I could hardly wait as I looked at my plate,
And my dinner adventure began.

First I climbed up Spaghetti Mountain,
All twirly and slippery to cross.
Then I dove in for a dangerous swim
In the lake called Tomato Sauce.

From there I marched daringly onward
Through a soft squooshy field of white bread,
Till the terrible jungle of Spinach Mungle
Lay on my path straight ahead.

I waded and sloshed through that jungle,
All yucchy and stringy and green.
Then I rounded a bend, and my trip reached its end
On the beautiful Hill of Ice Cream.

I had an adventure at dinner,
Exciting and scary and fun.
I explored and I ate all the things on my plate,
So my dinner adventure was done.

Hoots the Owl

Underneath the stars
Sitting all alone,
Playing quiet music
On his saxophone,
Hoots the Owl is happy
There beneath the moon.
He toots a gentle rhythm,
An owl-y kind of tune.
While you and I are sleeping,
His listeners gather near.
Lightning bugs and night birds
Huddle close to hear.
He plays for them till morning,
Until it's time to rest.
He puts his saxophone away
And heads back to his nest.
As you and I are waking
And early sunlight streams,
Hoots is softly sleeping
In the land of owl-y dreams.

How We Got Where We Were Going

Ernie took a bike.
Bert took a train.
Telly took a sled.
Grover took a plane.
Oscar came by taxi
And Prairie by canoe.

Cookie rode with Herry
On a camel built for two.
Snuffy took a ferry.
I took a bus.
And when we got there,
We all met us!

Under My Covers, Far Away

Under my covers, far away
In the kingdom of Sleepy Stars,
Bananafish play and balloon trees sway
And jitterbugs come in jars.
Turtles sing and bluebells ring
And pelicans strum guitars,
Under my covers, far away,
In the kingdom of Sleepy Stars.

While I'm
Sleeping

While I'm sleeping
Through the night
The things I love
Are out of sight.

My dog, my train,
My favorite bear
All go away,
I'm not sure where.

But morning comes,
I wake and then
The things I love
Are back again.

If the Moon Were
a Blueberry Pie

If the moon were a blueberry pie,
We could all eat dessert in the sky.
We'd jump on a rocket
With forks in our pocket
And drink milk from a cow flying by.